BLACK SUN

Black Sun

TOBY MARTINEZ DE LAS RIVAS

FABER & FABER

First published in 2018
by Faber & Faber Ltd
Bloomsbury House
74–77 Great Russell Street
London WC1B 3DA

Typeset by Hamish Ironside
Printed in England by Martins the Printers, Berwick-upon-Tweed

A CIP record for this book is available from the British Library

ISBN 978–0–571–33379–0

2 4 6 8 10 9 7 5 3 1

Acknowledgements

Acknowledgements are due to the editors of the following publications where versions of these poems first appeared: *Ambit, Eboracon, Tupelo Press, The Clearing, La Errante, Minerva, PRAC CRIT* and *New Walk*. I would like to offer my thanks to Simona Noli, Shane McCrae, James Byrne, Sandeep Parmar, Martha Sprackland, Luke Thompson and Karl O'Hanlon for their support, encouragement, tolerance and correspondence in recent times, as well as to my editors, Lavinia Singer and Matthew Hollis, for their patience and exceptional advice. Finally, I would like to express my deep gratitude to Dr Arin Keeble, Professor Simon James and Melanie Challenger for friendships which mean a great deal to me, and to Lucy Mercer for the same, together with her extensive and invaluable work on the text.

The mind seeks what is dead, since what is living escapes it
MIGUEL DE UNAMUNO

Contents

Very few are the precious things that remain precious
URSULA K. LE GUIN

and as a watch in the night
PSALM 90:4

I am sorry, I have been so long –
the angels have turned a little further
to watch across a field of broken statues
and the sun has fallen three thousand times.

The willow bends
So long the dragonfly has risen from its deep,
the mouse from its labour, the vole from its sleep,
the girl from her texting, the worm from its sheep,
the king from his castle and the castle from its keep.

i.m. J.F. 1978–2006, & to O.H.

And I know what news you are bearing,
your sob at my ear wearing
the shape of his body in the earth's cold springs –
but even there I hear a broken voice, singing.

Here is the ghost of a child I once knew
still playing among the withering harebells
& the gorgeous *moue* of the fairy flax.
I look beyond his bare golden head
to the kestrel that quarters the ramparts
& see a semblance of absolute love,
absolute mercy – at least a baffling, wild
joy – that, at least – in the watchfully poised
javelin of the head, the rapidity
of hér stoop & strike, hér failure, hér re-
lofting, the gaze that hungers into the spindle
without end: whose flowers are blood red,
whose roots drive down among the lost chieftains.
A lonely god waits for us in the earth.

Hunting Kestrel, Danebury

Come back through this glass darkly to a day
pell mell with leaves: silvery, emerald,
winged, tumbling: & the sun in its black sky.
Little man, as if asleep in the grass –
shadows touch the earth & lift as quickly,
the oceans of ash glitter & sweep them-
selves into foaming peaks, troughs of cloud   *The Trap*
deepen & loom above you as mercy may –

& I see again the whole legendary
estate of my life condensed to this moment's
triumph – crudely sensual, as if drowning
in amber, golden mop of hair ablow –
as the white rat breaks into its sunlight
& my wadcutter is singing through the air.

The next day, fierce gusts still blew. You staggered
as if wasted – I had no idea, then –
from a deep-shouldered shove that made no headway
into pockets of air drained of resistance.
You came into my arms, I into yours;
we were driven like leaves across the lawn.

An exhilarance, a fine careless joy,   *The Great Storm*
consecutive crashes of wheelie bins tumbling.
My hood trembled with hidden power,
your voice, even at the full, lost in the roar
that tossed the crowns of trees about their axes,
shattered the bullfinch in the orchard,
rained down. Heaven in such earnest, I thought –
nothing I love can withstand this onslaught.

A simple & plaintive cry into history –
for the illusion of security
that was the past & will be the past once
more when the foundations are broken down
& all things stand reconciled to their first
natures, when the lamb lies beside the tiger
& the bullfrog is crushed in the way.

Address to my Children
i.m. J. E. Bullen,
25 March 1916–17 March 2010

He would lift his eyes past mine to the hills
'. . . from whence cometh my help . . .' & I could not
detect if that was statement or question.
No hint of irony nor deference
in a voice stripped of its northern inflections –
lovely chirr of the Tiger Moth
that is lost to you, my little sons.

Between the firing range & the lagoon
turquoise crowns of sea holly prick the sky,
a stand of gorse anoints the headland
with ash & the recollection of glory.
No motion in the cold grey lapse of water
where stretches of weed extend like hair
into a black shelving-off of shingle,   *Fleet*
& none here, as sleek clouds shroud the bluff.
I had been desperate for a word, a sign,
a coincidence, a kind of simultaneity,
a touch, a little whisper, anything –
would have waded into the still waters
like the glaring heron. Somewhere the sun,
its great blind eye shaking with laughter, is.

Night

The hard cold face of the flint shines
as I pass the chapel, its vacant windows
glow – but in the dark behind them I know
the Sunday school desks still stand in line
beneath a thin patina of dust & moths,
waiting for the consummation of the days
as the seasons deepen, & the butterflies   *The Deconsecrated Chapel, Wildhern*
lay down their wings like brittle wreaths.

Let there be no arrogance nor deceit
in me – only a stark light the moon casts
across wheat in absolute monochrome,
& the fields as if crested with white foam
where, a broken leveret slumped in its claw,
the owl flickers across the haunted mow.

Dawn

Set down once & for all in this white earth
the light pink inflorescence of *Thalictrum*
like an airburst candled in pearls of dew,
the bipinnate leaves gathered in deep shade,
the flowerheads thrust into early sun –
as ornate, as delicately woven
as needle lace, or like the ghostly aureole

Thalictrum 'Elin', Wildhern

that heralds God & the moon in frost.
Unpetalled, scentless, barely present in time,
as gas igniting & a faint cluster of stars,
the flowers exhale beneath the threshold of
hearing, constellate their little season
with pinpricks of joy, suffer the tempest, fall,
& sleep untroubled through wintry soil.

In my kingdom it is winter forever.
The snow falls & there is no time nor day –
no distinction between things, no compare,
no flaw to taint our rudimentary clay.

The falcon has flown away with history,
the bullfinch sheathed in ice & snow, the bare
branch shall never know its May,
nor husband teach the vanity of despair.

At Lullington Church/To My Daughter

Nothing disturbs its peaceful sleep, no dream
of life, no hope, no falsifying dawn
alleviates the blank space within the frame –
no words to speak, no beauty to adorn.

Until she wakes & finds herself alone,
you are her rock, Lord. Lord, you are stone.
Lully, Lulley, Lully, Lulley.

Abhor the body of my adulthood,
deep in its changes, gradually humbled;
that can barely speak its loss to itself
or look within the green of its own eyes
where objects lie as if on the surface
of a mirror – sharply resolved, redefined,
counterfeit – a merciless, cold rigor
that is in me as it is in the earth.

But still the days shift despite themselves;
& how hard it becomes not to repeat
a jaded metaphor – that nature
in its dream of spring, its riots of growth,
the flower's deep corolla might be
the image of his love's blind insurrection.

Hope/Against Nature

My neighbours cry out as if in pain, *¡oh!*
¡oh! ¡oh! & doves clatter into the air.
Late evening, heat, the streets full of strollers
& elegant *viejos* resting hands & chin
upon slim mother-of-pearl-tipped canes,
the lightly oiled curls of hair at each nape
fixed as they turn, one to another,   *Raptus*
in amused complicity to wink & yawn.
But something else lies within that rapture.
A yearning, a hole, a want. A question
without answer, prayer with no response –
as if a mouth had opened into the pit
of stars & the brilliant darkness cried out
that I might also possess it: their lack.

Despite the shit we've put each other through –
& even though the trap of your teeth
snapped at my throat as the withering flash
of your palm opened & fell again
& again & I bent my head down beneath
that bitter rain – still I find
the days that lengthen with you more precisely   *The Durable Fire*
themselves than I ever imagined.
Through this deep rage that distorts our bodies;
through hurt, betrayal, the difficult births
in search of some myth that might prove more
durable to our selves than each other –
still you step to this page's bare panopticon,
belovèd, contemptuous of ruin.

The starkly intimate moment you pee
in front of me for the first time – the glass
vague with condensation as your eyes
frame themselves in the mirror's stare.

Turning, I catch a look I've not seen
before – half apologetic, half exposed,
both at ease & on edge as you compose   *Portrait*
yourself & undo the black ritual gown.

A deftness in you, neither innocence
nor calculation – more a sharp instinct
for the complicity that grants assent,
your vulnerable strength a clairvoyance

as you wind the paper round your hand,
then draw it between your legs & stand.

my dove

Lost my life to a dark dream. Lost my life
in the rain out beyond Simonsburn
& Bywell where our manners fell away
& we struggled for purchase in the wet earth.

Where a wet coat & cold adoration
& nothing. Where the sun, withdrawing, stares
beneath the ragged fringe of the cloudbase,   *Tender Image*
the shining fields retted with dew.

Kiss me on the mouth & on my open eyes, *my dove*
& bury me deep within that portion
of the earth that is given over to the dead
where these manifold beauties accrue:

our absence lies in the grass forever,
the crocus is broken. World without end,

In the kingdom there shall be a perfect silence, as in my defence. Sunlight stood in the orchard among the trees and broken espaliers. Something cried out in the darkness beyond the walls.

I have come to stand at your border
in the darkness where invisible things suffer
& the golden windows of the last estate
cast proprietary glances on the earth.
Where the bailiff parks up with his sandwich
& the burnt-out car is mercifully at rest.
Hermosa, let me try a final   *England*
octave turning south into a wind that stubbornly
flitters through torn pennants of sacking,
purrs in the steel tubes of the gate;
that drives each ponderous & docile cloud
slowly out across the State that is only
an image of the body inviolate,
the nation that extends through all time & space.

I will wake to see clouds
This is a song of annihilation
where the falcon draws out its staggering cry
above the city grown numb with pleasure.
Somehow it has deserved this. Not the people –
or not only the people, or if the people
then, *my love*, you & I among them – but the battering
displays of pride, the concupiscent eye

Avenging & Bright

bent inward w/ súch deep longing.

(After watching the peregrines at South Bank, hunting)

Her perpetual false day eradicates the stars;
what has fallen to her stays fallen.
Did we, too, walk in those great parks at leisure
admiring her magnanimity & climate?
Black sun – rise in glory & begin to shine
as the rock dove cries its expiation.
gathering behind the sun

One day, I shall have to give an account
of *my* self with my knees couched
in dirt & the great cities tumbling like stars.
If not to hím, then to that portion of *my*
self that holds the rod & sits in judgement.
Out in the snowstorm, & the lake
like a field of burning heather, beautiful.   *To a Metropolitan Poet*
Christ, I can't stand those popinjays,
so deep in theory, so ostentatiously tolerant.
Always wanting to interrogate
shit or excavate shit, when what they mean
is read shit. This is so fucking point-
less, *Tobe*. You are not theirs, finally, or even
hís, that sees beauty where no other can.

I have searched my whole life for a studied
artifice in which the image can neither
wilt nor grow, but is fixed like a rose in ether –
la naturaleza muerta: the dead body
we enact our fears & tenderness upon –
coddle; sing hymns to that the disregarding god
of our fathers might finally cherish; turn:
& return alone to a house of blood.
This is hers. The ornate hairdo & frozen tears,
the whole retroactive dream of the glory
of Spain, our House in the days of its power –
& in a sullen ring around the eye, a yellow
bruise raised in defiance as she sinks
through cold water like the crippled *Oquendo*.

House of Blood

*i.m. Irene Martinez de las Rivas,
née Webb, 1907–2004*

*i.m. José María Martinez de las
Rivas, 1850–1913*

To know that all of this might be empty
or without meaning, or the meaning
not meant for us, or that we shall never see
face to face in our second beginning.

To know that we might finally go down
with *sed omnes una manet nox* burnt
into our hearts, all our little hopes flown
as the dawn & every lesson unlearned.

To know – & still to resist a last despair;
to return from the six years of exile
& begin your lecture, 'Decíamos ayer . . .'

Not to allow doubt to corrupt the heart's
native charity, as into the dream
of a final sleep you go, broken moderate.

The Same Night Waits for Everyone
i.m. Miguel de Unamuno,
d. 31 December 1936

My putative great-great-cousin lies dead
as a rat in the snow, a thick circle
of blood crowning, like a halo, his head.
He seems in my imagining immortal

in that pose as a foetus hunched around
its wound, the snow golden in a blank sea
of light as half the Carlist infantry
struggles to rise to its knees & the ground

Still Life
i.m José María Martinez de las Rivas
y Villabaso, d. 28 December 1938

shakes so deeply the Ebro floods its banks.
Bare trees – tranches of ice on the river
break up as the geese with great low honks
flying in torn formations here & there

escape those limbs, his open mouth as silent
as the Earth's, possessing nothing it is brought.

It was as though I had been in bed for weeks in a dark room . . .

Her nipples tickling the grass in a shower
of moths, the bull-terrier slips by.
Songs sing, tweets arrive with brazen éclat,
the high-pitched bang of an old telephone
slammed into its cradle rings out
across the square with horns & a fine
spray from the fountain clouding the cool air.

Breakfast, Plaza de la Magdalena,
Córdoba

In the courtyard of my racial memory
there is a well cut into the rock
opening like a mouth pocked with green ferns.
It reaches down to a pool of black water
that quivers as the slow drops drip. Beside it,
as tall as it is deep, a lemon tree.
When will you rise, self, like the sun & see?

Up there, where the darkness is – is always,
does not abate, nor lighten, attenuate –
an owl revolves, strung by the neck in rings
of wire. A gorgeous ruff now mocked with blood,
one claw hooked through the noose, one wing let fall
as if to reach for earth, one still spread wide.
& I marvelled as it swung its *glimme*   *Allegory of the Church/Hanged Owl*
there so gently – round & round, side to side –
each gauzy breath, each faded breeze
in feathers toned to silent pleas
blessed its poise, its lack, the one visible
dead eye a black disc through cloud, the cold ●
tundra of a mind imperfectly at ease.
o.   Elizabeth. The Lord turns like a lamp in his sleep.
     Elizabeth –

Though I am afraid, I am not afraid.
Blue cables of lightning leap from the hills.
The hills go white, then black, then white,
then kneel into the towering cumuli.

A sudden breeze like Kreutzer Sonata,
allegro with lovely phrases of joy
blushes in the leaves of the guelder rose –
the water at St Mary Bourne is still.

*Allegory of the State/September
in St Mary Bourne*

A collared dove lies beneath the corn,
cold-eyed abandoned priestess of summer
sheared open beneath a fractured wing.

A thin cloud of flies attend her,
sleek abdomena pulsing in the wind –
their fruit lies deep in the penetralium.

To come to terms with them not as you wish
them to be, Tobe, but as they really are.
To come to terms, at last, with yourself & find
behind the priggishness & *vergüenza*
this constant, bitter dialogue with failure
that is manhood in its blossoming.
The winters fulfil their stern & beautiful   *Winter Parable/The Others*
intent in you; a trail of gore winding
through the frost from the stream of living
waters to the corner of an outhouse
where a shape lies bent about its wound –
do not turn yr face from this, though the háwk
withers the cruel point of íts beak in you,
& the early lambs cry like wolves in the fold.

I fear and hope with such rapid transition.
May has come to the heart, & still the starred
& elegant pasque flowers in the yard,
her violets edged with white & glowing yolk
etch in frost a delicate baroque.
Flurries of rain are all about – then sun, then rain,
then aquarelle of morning, then sun again.

What remains of this when all else is gone –   *At Lullington Church/Idumæa*
you, the rain, yr daughter & yr sons?
More than a memory anchored to the rock –
if you can bear the lightness of his yoke;
more than flesh which kept its watch & guard
through the long night of his Word.

Thief, turn yr head,
yr Lord will not let you lie in bed.

The memory of night is brought to its knees
above the minarets & whitewashed walls.
Now the sun rises like a disc of clay
as each separate shadow lengthens & kneels
into itself, bells cry out, the *afilador*
blows his syrinx through these wild orders.
Outside my window, the dead images
resurrect – a troupe of swifts, black-headed, chaste,
feint & roll, blur, bustle against the ridges
& I push them faster across this waste
until one breaks out, dives among the alleys,
twists, appears, disappears, goes free.
A quick guilt pulses. Its careless measures
whistle through my sorrow's inertia.

A May Morning in Córdoba
i.m. Alison Martinez de las Rivas,
née Holmes,
14 October 1951–26 March 2015

There is a city triumphant in the clouds –
its cold, unshakeable flank of light
touches the spire of Salisbury cathedral
& conjures a fan vault from the air.
Life gathers there without motion – white rooks
lift their bodies from the beeches & oaks,
the crown of the sycamore buttresses
the light, the sky, the whole stilled society.

Remembering the Rex Whistler Memorial Prism, Salisbury Cathedral

No ostentation in sorrow, & no tears.
Dignity is finally this resolute,
insular silence – the self leant upon
the self, as this slowly turning block of glass
in which the angles of reflection
make whole the emptiness of each image.

For my father

And you, who swept away the temples of stone
& the Hierarchy, the old courtesies,
the mannered, blind, intractable reserve –
what god did you leave us that suffers
as we suffer: is lost, consigned, abandoned, *in silence*
your suave faces fixed in the rapturous
cold light of screens tweeting into the hole?

Culture/Apocalypse

Isabel, the three thousand days since we spoke
seem to rise all at once, like a black sun.
Let the rats nose from their burrows into its night
as we all must, you & me & Oli   *starry*
hand in hand, kissing each other's white faces,
& crying out with Paul φρόνημα τῆς σαρκὸς –
I sing what is Greek, & eternal.
As do my hands

Sodom? I summoned my heartland under the sun's blinding rim. Nothing. No Lux Aeterna. Will you know when the time for your littleness has come, and a light betrays the walls of your

the resurrection of the state

a little . . . night music . . .

. . . sand dune surrounded by pure nothingness . . .

W. G. SEBALD

So that I shall no longer tarnish with my fingers
Bells smash through the day: lauds, vespers, High Mass.
Stiff figures kneeling as if into a storm
maintain, like old lovers, an awkward peace.

Devotions

The moon's bow curves deeply into the sky.
I hold myself here face to face with the worm
& the darkness is ablaze upon me.

Shadows move in the slipstream of our eyes –
it is ourselves we nearly catch blowing
from the bough, held for a moment in the wind,
then – *whoosh!* – the furnace of late summer
is crackling again with thin gold leaves,
scrub oaks wince from hills where earth turns
the colour of wine, the stones hunch,
egrets with legs trailing like anchor ropes
stall through heaven with a sail's inertia.
Breaching the last crest onto the floodplain
the sea proclaims its sudden infinity:
cobalt blue on the far horizon softening
to aquamarine, sky-blue, blue of washed-out
euphoria, the white surf crowning its moment.
Santa María de la Asunción –
her darkness grows behind us to counter
this light, her stillness this ceaseless motion.   *Caños de Meca*
How many miles since her clean lines pierced
the day like nails, the reticent silver
of the tabernacle glowing through shadows,
& the priest itchily shifting from foot
to foot sleepy in alb & chasuble?
Slowly we descend from Conil, the bright
walls of sister villages signalling
in unison across the bay; no virtue
there in a softer palette, the scorched grass
& a glitter of terns above the headland –
Trafalgar, those imperial fathoms.
What am I withholding? I barely know
myself. These are the bones of a memory
covered in sand the dull green armoured crab
daintily exploits with each jointed foot –
this is not how it was, not how it was,
& after all there was nothing, is nothing

but this desert where the will lies in its flesh,
thoughts trace hemicycles in the sand.
The sun will go down like a torch slowly
showering the surf in a torrent of sparks,
spilling through the cases of cicadas
that cling to the bark in their emptiness,
people emerge laughing & kissing,
their shapes lost again among the beachgrass.
But lift your eyes & lift your voice up
as the day fails to the stark white lighthouse
on the headland, the beam of its single eye
groping out across the strait to Africa.
What are these exclamations that flare
in its path like words given in witness –
the bodies of gulls raising their sharp cries
as they pass into the silence of night?
The bougainvillea wilts in its glance,
breakers shudder to a halt on the fringe
of shore where a couple bursts into brief,
dark substance & the day is far spent. *Luke 24:29*
Still a murmur from the bar beneath the palms,
the brilliant lamentation of ringtones.

Landscape bares itself like the totality
of hís love as the evangelists conceived it –
an olive tree twists in its private dusk
then stands still an awful second
as the brief bars of light go scurrying by.
So smooth, so smooth in its carriage
the train hisses, suave gesture of contempt
ploughing through orchards & under mountains.
Time ungathers, then refolds in its wake
like a trail through the aftermath,
the stands whispering past in a blind rush
to Aragon, to the high places
deep in their shifting tides of snow, or
cold at their foot, the sea's austerity.

Diptych: Córdoba – Barcelona

A dead calm will litter the bay, the ferry
in its harbour glittering like a bauble.
All my pleasure is a kind of acquiescence
to the helpless thrust of the journey –
the train dividing the darkness from itself
& flinging its glow to the verges
where the olives diminish row on row
& I can sit & watch them go.
No longer read with the same fierce hunger
or belief in the power of words
to summon mercy or mitigate our loss,
though there is a line I recall in Machado –
Todo pasa y todo queda:
all things pass away, & all things remain.

Look across to the citadel on the hill
where you stayed – & stay – every summer.
I dream the speckled blue corollae
of your eyes falling acquisitively upon
the bare shoulders of strangers & lightening,
maybe, with a dead image of me.
The bodies that were ours – sober, intense,
courteously deferent to each other
through the days of our unconsummated
wedding hang above me like smoke in the rain.
Something – loss or failure or the distant
intimacies of regret – fades away
with the shreds of those fantastic beings.
I do not hate the life I have chosen.

Diptych: Cortona

A stormhead is blowing over the ridge,
massive needles of sunlight pierce the crown
& wheel away to drape the far hillside
in exquisite tapestries of rain.
The desolate face of the scarp turns white
with joy, then wavers & dissolves as if
sinking through deep water.
I turn away into the crenellated
dark & walk along Renaissance alleys,
chaste stone reiterating the hunger
of the days in its flank, back to the church
dressed in baroque ironies that stands
in its silent square at the end of all roads,
since it is what we are: broken desire.

Gone you are nothing, Né, a dream whose name
I rarely spoke, a (*cloud*) dissolving like flesh.
Time is only a kind of space that grows
& exerts itself like a fever &
we burn. Bells clash in air, little titans. *v*
Time is only a kind of space
like the burnt zero of ground swelling behind
a ring of fire as it steps through dry scrub
& the vulnerable bright things cling to stems
with awe & sharp chirrups of distress. *v*
It is like nothing (as this is like nothing)
& that is its meaning: to mean no-
thing, to arrive nowhere with its fine words
already spoken & its hands empty. *iv*

The dead are in us, Né – slowly, slowly
raising their bald heads from the soil, slowly
magnifying their colours like the vivid
puffs of oleander blowing south
from the central reservation. *v*
The black kites drift over, something deadly
& angelic in their half-swept wings;
cars grope toward the emptiness that lies
upon the horizon as the road
narrows to a point, or turn & glide up *v*
to that white confection straddling the hill
where the sun scours the earth to clay
& the devastated strays wander
with blank, defeated eyes – Fernan Nuñez. *iv*
                              Espejo

*Hey. So anyway, I got this joke. Two
guys out hunting. One of them collapses.
It doesn't look like he's breathing & his eyes
are glazed over. The other guy whips
out his cellphone & dials 999 & screams,
'Help! I think my friend is dead. What can I do?'
So the operator says, 'Look, stay calm.
The first thing we need to do is make sure
he really is dead, okay. Can you do
that for me?' 'Sure,' says the guy. Silence
as he puts the phone down on a rock
then BLAM, the operator hears a gunshot.
The guy picks up the phone. 'Right. Now what?'
No? Okay. So, a seal walks into a club.*

Allegory of Fate

*But Sssh; everything is so far away
& long ago. Somewhere in the boy you see
the man; somewhere in the man, the boy.
Who will I say I am on that day
when there are none beside me & I slip
between the hedges to the Throne & death?
D'you remember we found a fallen swift?
Her puny flutterings in San Agustin –
& after coffee there was the heat & a walk
& (I am talking only to you) I said
what I said on the Vial & will not recant?
Do you remember the freak black of her eye,
the slim white gorget on her throat?
Even through this night, I cleave to you.*

Will I ever see you in England? Her deep,
assuaging greens all year multiplying
their tones violently as a triolet?
Will I ever see you in England, walking
in the garden where smoke quells the branches
& the bemes of daie divide or refract
like calyces clutching their flowers, her deep
abiding greens all year gathering *viii*
& deepening like the bow of a cello? Ah,
yes, *per violoncello*; our bodies
& the world; our bodies that are the world.
Né, my body stands open like a door
you can walk through – & what is incarnate
in it is what is incarnate in the earth, *vi*

my love, withering my self & my nation,
devolving to my children their little deaths;
that eats the world & its frail gods
like a (*cloud*), like a worm in its bowel,
like a black sun rising in the west. *v*
Here is Belle de Crécy kneeling in dews
as the Black Prince gave thanks with Chandos,
cerise pink softening to parma violet,
& the broken rose-canes nose-down in turf
like the mouths of the ribauldequin. *v*
Love, I have looked for you my whole life –
will I ever see you in England?
Her deep greens the bed of our union?
My sons shall grow in a headless kingdom. *iv*

Determinedly light: my whole tone here,
¿vale? The table I so loved has gone
though the cypress still burns in the corner
of the yard like a black candle.
A bird sped out of it. I was shaking.
But I mean not just my hands – my being;
my whole being like a city under siege.
Darkness & the heat radiating from
the walls. 'Dear Goldberg, do play me one
of my variations.' He does. Triumphantly
disembodied across 250 years.
Let there be no sleep this side of dawn;
already half drunk con anhelo,
reclining like nudes on our little poufs.

Allegory of Parting

Will you walk into the kingdom with me
where the sky is like chalcedony
& on the field of cloth of gold there stands
an altar with the king as celebrant?
There are lutes & drums & clarions,
& Bach's Suiten für Violoncello
& the city beyond the altar is built
of white stone trimmed with adamant.
Shall we neck in the sun? Get a little
high, touch, adore, whisper, drag deep raking
scratches down each other's bare sides?
The great lords all kneeling beside
their oriflammes & plunging destriers,
the harnesses 'set full of trembling spangs . . .'

Nedelya

You are my Sabbath in the long cool grass
beneath the olives in Asomadilla
where the mirador stares out across the city
to the hills that are beginning to parch. *iv*
Sabbath on a Thursday morning
with our phones set to dark mode & silent;
the great sad stars waiting behind
a vault of blue, the slow mania of swifts. *iv*
Later the housewives will come with their quiffed
little dogs on leads closely following
in step like children with wistful
glances back to the jacaranda's pall of flowers,
& the fat men that go to sleep with such
patient, stern alacrity in the grass. *vi*

Né

How will I find you in that other life
that will be ours, when our flesh is not this flesh
& the eyes I know shall be different eyes?
How will I find you in a country
so utterly discomposed – trees with no roots
burning in the mind, birds whose names
I do not know spread across a vault
of stars that will not fade in their constellations? *viii*
Who will come to us out of the garden
to set my self-knowledge beside
your self-knowledge & our mouths together? *iii*
Who will wipe away our tears,
where loss cowers beneath the beech hedge
& every day is like a thousand years? *iii*

*Here's another one. There was an English-
man, an Irishman & a Scotsman. No,
I'm kidding. Hurt me, if you want.
Dig your nails in. Your teeth. Whatever.
The moon is rising like a white sun
sneaking crafty little sideways glances
at us as it scuttles over the roof
of the church – bald eternal miserabilist.
I have an eye, over your shoulder,
for the cars like boxes of drowned light
scouring the cobbles, & the passers-
by peering up at us, their cold white faces
hard set with tasteful little frowns.
Fuck them. My hands smell of you & I purr.*

Allegory of Desire

*Shall I walk, in the end, alone like Arwen
Undómiel through Laurelindórenan?
There is nothing there, now, to keep any-
thing from dying & the leaves have
fallen for the first time & are everywhere.
Desire has its own species & top-
ography. I don't think I could name anything
there, or say which are hills & which
valleys; nor how I got here, nor the way out.
I do not want the way out. The day
that breaks, dividing us, I hate, though
I see you in the newness of its light.
The cars fire up in the cool street – do not
leave stay a while yet a little longer.*

In the marches of his night

A black tarpaulin like the crumpled wings
of seraphim all fallen in one
corner of the field, the yellow stubble
aglow – the rick is burning again in my dreams.
I wake into darkness, reach for you
& find your shoulder beneath my fingers,
your dependable, deep inhalations
coming & going like a life's dynamic
tread between being born & dying,
between the day our sober lips first touched
& what must come: a slow crucifixion.
We have loved each other – haven't we, you
& I? Through the minor difficulties,
the brittleness of feeling, days of complaint?   *Diptych: Waking at 4 a.m.*
Laughed together, consoled each other,
sat through the night, maintained our privacies?
So why, your hand beneath mine, do I
still glimpse in darkness this dancing light?
Look – there goes G.W weeping in frustration,
& I have come in a borrowed car to see
the disconsolate insurance agent,
the woods in silence, the flames in the trees.
Stars, go out: your blithe little faces
do not fit here – they are nothing beside
the pillar of fire that turns my body
orange & black between the pines that wait
to burn at the field's edge & the western
sky's rhetoric of abandonment.

Faded kingdom: the swallows bear their blued
bodies low over the green. They are grace
itself, snatching a raindrop from the air,
mowing a swathe through clouds of *Diptera*.
Nothing will rescue this from the city –
they come so arch, my generation,
so French with irony, *mwah, mwah, mwah*,
up for the weekend with endless profile
updates: me at the march, me at the shoot,
me with a glorious dead light rising
in the eastern sky that is the moon casting
its gaze of deep anxiety between
the crowns of the beech trees, the river's thick
oils at midnight running with white fire.

Diptych: At Matfen/
Address to My Daughter

Heri et hodie ipse et in saecula

Always the same. Whether I hold or whether
I do not, the centre does not wither –
it stays & stays through each changing season:
'. . . no variableness, nor shadow of turning . . .'
In us there is a turning: here, in these
collapsing bodies, in these minds, these hearts
like the swallow switching its aim between
targets, its manifold inconstancies
reaching out in despair to touch nothing
but the world's own mutability.
Our beautiful & tender words – these, too,
are failing. Between the salon leftists
& the slaughterhouse of capital,
keep your wild hope in salvation's blindness.

Oh, how frightened I was!

Doves court on the sill in winter light
with bristling breasts & sumptuous trains in tow,
now gorgeous, now abject, filthy in white,
a last dance of the day before vespers.
He, a Hakluyt's pale Francis, bows, parades
a gallant ruff. She, coy, gazing upward,
might convulse in laughter – instead maintains
her organised desires, the ritual decorum.
Behind coloured glass casting its glory
into the high, cold darkness of the church
I watch their stately courtesies embrace
a mutual violence of adoration,
wings that thrash through gradations of violet
& gold, a deep blue encompassing Ararat.

Crucifixion, Winter, Córdoba

What covenant might equal or surpass
the burning rainbow that surmounts the dead
like a kestrel perched upon its pierced prey
but this radical idiom of passion?
Like a rising tide, the pure, ahistorical
light that breaks in waves above Calvary
breaks here, too, upon the familiar
gaunt frame of his alterity.
& you, wandering among the empty aisles
late in the day of yr perpetual winter;
will you turn yr face away from those eyes
closed in loss, the collarbone aglow
in a final flash of sun – that stir a culpable
tenderness in you, desiring & fearing?

Now the dragonfly breaks through the grey
shell of its body on a stalk of mace
& climbs into the world on that burnt black
flowerhead bobbing in the pretty wind.
The river flows, her deep dark oils & swirls
swell up & slide away; whose waters
shadow little depths; whose thin green weeds
unfurl their hair like a lost Ophelia.
There is a rainbow rising slowly through
the multiple facets of his single eye,
a wind that dandles the white of his wings,
a blind & burning cloud upon the hill.
He dries – his Arctic blues & molten golds
solidify around copper lamé.

Crucifixion with Dragonfly

In *Corpus Hypercubus* I cannot see
if the curled palms are really pierced by nails,
or if the crown of thorns still sits atop –
jauntily atop – the unrefusing head.
Hé has gone free of that dread assemblage;
there is only the beauty of the body
released back to the infinite peace of space,
& the sky blackening over Port Lligat.
No time redounds there – we, watching, are time   *my love*
incarnate: breaking & broken, suffering
all things between the sea's distant breath
& the stare of the Magdalene until
our final cry that is a cry of pain
shatters the night with its *Laudate Dominum*.

Here are the crucified: I know some of them.
Some are being crucified as I speak.
& all, little daughter, step in their turn
to that sorrow that blossoms in the crown.
Are these, Love, the εἴδωλα of History –
the threshing floor in Matthew three twelve,
or a memory of no memory
where the dead instruct the living in hope
& these children genuflecting before
the golden statues begin their journey
into the same ignorance I know
so intimately, those familiar terrors
where the great blind god is a god of death,
& the image is always broken?

Crucifixion, August, Lullington

I have dreamed that body a thousand times,
the death that rolls across it an eclipse,
a black sun fringed with burning coronae.
In whose self-denial the bleak orbit
of a whole culture adapts itself to hope,
& more than hope – to history, worlds beyond this,
knowledge, carnality, love, joy, the dawn
that breaks upon the city of the dead.
I do not hate the world; I know it
a thin wish that each small thing be restored
to itself in final reconciliation,
the swallow at Lullington re-angling her wings
among dandelions in the yard at dusk –
my children, too, step up from the wreckage.
It was as dark as night inside the wolf

'The swallows began their display at dusk,
streaming through rain: one curtseyed on the wing –
a move of such eloquence – & plucked
a drop from the air; another sank, sank, sank,
to trail its beak through the still water
of the loch, then accelerated out
over the bay with imaginary
engine noise until I lost her in the blue . . .'
This last summer creeps north in a drizzle
of stars; a boat rests in the harbour.
West there is nothing but the moon's pale track
in the sea glittering & glittering
like fame all the way to Newfoundland
& a rumour of bears on the shoreline.

Diptych: A Holiday in the Western Isles
i.m. John Derry, DFC
i.m. Anthony Richards
& 29 bystanders
d. 6 September 1952, Farnborough

When the long day rises, the resolute eye
at the binoculars takes it all in –
bull-necked fulmars, the white terns helmeted
in black rearing over the headland,
kittiwakes that cry out their own shrill names.
Inland, gaudy shimmers of heat shake
the middle distance, a violet daze of heather
at the margin dances with butterflies.
Will the winter never come, her naked
cupidity, frost muzzling the spurs,
the intense chorus of the gorseflowers
setting the earth alight with yellow candles?
Silence in the wood, where the raptor
thrusts among branches hooded with snow?

Will we be ourselves again? In the cold
January morning? Will our bodies
reach toward us stripped of their failures,
set themselves about us like ermine
in their opulence & *bobaunce*?
Will we touch as we touched for the first time
among the hours – drunk, in the stairwell,
at odds with our lives for no reason,
my tongue touching your tongue shyly, at first,
your fingers bending back my fingers?
As we passed beneath the skylight, the clouds
slashed through with cloth of gold slid by
real slow up there like an armada,
& the winter birds sang into each other.

Diptych: The Alnmouth Resurrection

Will we stand as we stood among the jeans
& crumpled shirts, our hands clothed
with flesh like charmeuse, tipped with nails
that rake, the whiteness of your skin
like the cuisses of frost armouring
the stems of wild celery at Alnmouth;
sun that pales even as it climbs to its throne;
a thin sleet beginning to turn ever more
viciously from, or unto, the east,
the bright houses sewn to their little mump
where a tongue of rock reaches out
to the slakes, the slakes to the sea, the sea
to the pole, & the pole to a final, cold
heaven where there is no night, & no dawn?
The bright steel of your power

like the skin of Anne of Bohemia lying in State
wrapped in her arms – two sable eagles,
a raging lion, queue forchée, argent, crowned

or, fleur-de-lys – & Richard, 'wild with grief',
smashed Arundel to the ground for his sneer
in front of all the lords & magnates.

His love for us is like a boar lance. Stoned again in the thin rain. Can't tell you how it'll feel, to be alone here when the black sun steps clear of the horizon. To have, and then not to have.

ciega
vul.cor

Notes

The italicised superscriptions in '*i.m. J.F. 1978–2006, & to O.H.*' and '*Culture/ Apocalypse*' are from the song 'In the End' by Peter Hammill.

'*Hunting Kestrel, Danebury*': Danebury Ring, near Andover in Hampshire, is an Iron Age hill fort, excavated between 1969 and 1988 by Professor Barry Cunliffe.

'*Great Storm*': It is hard to overstate the violence of the Great Storm of 15–16 October 1987. Millions of mature trees were destroyed in the UK, and many landscapes changed radically overnight. For a short but intimate account of the storm and its aftermath, see W. G. Sebald, *Rings of Saturn*, chapter IX.

'*The Durable Fire*': The title is from the last verse of *Walsingham* by Sir Walter Raleigh.

'*House of Blood*': In Spanish, the term for 'still life' is *la naturaleza muerta* – 'dead nature'. José María Martinez de las Rivas was a Spanish industrialist and senator from the Basque country who was instrumental in spurring the economic development of Vizcaya. In partnership with Sir Charles Palmer of Newcastle-upon-Tyne, he established a large shipbuilding works in Bilbao where three major Spanish vessels were built: *Infanta Maria Teresa*, *Vizcaya* and *Almirante Oquendo*. All three were sunk at the battle of Santiago de Cuba on 3 July 1898. The family possessed the titles of Marquès de Mudela, Conde de Oñate and Duque de Najera. José María was expelled from the Asociacíon de Patrones Mineros de Vizcaya for siding with the workers he employed in the strike of 1910.

'*Miguel de Unamuno y Jugo*': Basque poet and philosopher, twice rector of Salamanca University. Under the dictatorship of General Miguel Primo de Rivera he was removed and went into exile, returning to his post in 1930 after an absence of six years and, so the story goes, beginning his first lecture back with the phrase, 'As we were saying yesterday . . .' His religious thought is beset by intense hope and intense anxiety, perhaps best seen in his novela *Saint Manuel Bueno, Martyr*. The Latin is from Horace, Odes 1, 28: 'sed omnes una manet nox / et calcanda semel via leti' ('but one night waits for everyone, and we must all tread the road to death').

'*Still Life*': The Catalonia Offensive, 23 December 1938–26 January 1939.

'*Breakfast, Plaza de la Magdalena, Córdoba*': The traditional Córdobese house is arranged around a patio, somewhat different from our idea of the word in English. Generally, it resembles a small flagged or cobbled courtyard, often containing a deep well and a lemon or grapefruit tree. The facade and most important architectural features of the house are internal – the exterior of the house is a simple blind wall. The *patio* is Islamic in origin.

'*At Lullington Church/Idumæa*': The title is a reference to Charles Wesley's hymn, which begins, 'And am I born to die / To lay this body down', and ends, 'Waked by the trumpet's sound / I from my grave shall rise / And see the Judge with glory crowned / And see the flaming skies.' There are several recordings of this hymn available. One of the most beautiful is a version by the German singer-songwriter Pantaleimon on the soundtrack to the 2006 Cam Archer film *Wild Tigers I Have Known*. The superscription is from *The Italian*, by Ann Radcliffe.

'*A May Morning in Córdoba*': The knife-sharpener ('*afilador*') cruises slowly from street to street on an old motorbike with a motorized whetstone fixed on the back. He plays a piercing, sometimes haunting tune on a pan flute to notify customers of his presence.

'*Culture/Apocalypse*': The Greek ('*phronema tes sarkos*') is from Romans 8:6, and means 'the mind bent upon the flesh.' The beginning of the KJV verse runs, 'For to be carnally minded is death.' I first encountered this phrase in T. A. Noble, 'Original Sin and The Fall: Definitions and a Proposal' in R. J. Berry and T. A. Noble (eds), *Darwin, Creation and the Fall: Theological Challenges* (Apollos, 2009).

The italicised fragments at the beginning of '*Devotions*' and the end of '*The Alnmouth Resurrection*' are from 'Resolve' by Louise Bogan.

'*Allegory of Fate*': 'Time is only a kind of space' is taken from H. G. Wells, *The Time Machine*.

'*Allegory of Parting*': 'beme of daie' is from Thomas Chatterton's 'Eclogue the Second,' and was also used by Barry MacSweeney in a poem, though I cannot locate which. I do recall the line, however: 'Inside this poem there is a beme of daie.' The superscription was a favourite motto of Edward III. The quotation in the minor sonnet is from Polydore Vergil's account of the meeting of Henry VIII and Francis I at the Field of the Cloth of Gold.

'*Allegory of Desire*': cf. 2 Peter 3:8-9: 'But, beloved, be not ignorant of this one thing, that one day is with the Lord as a thousand years, and a thousand years as one day' (KJV).

'*Crucifixion, Winter, Córdoba/Crucifixion Scene, August, Lullington*': The italicised fragments are from Vera Southgate's version of 'Little Red Riding Hood'.

'*Crucifixion with Dragonfly*': *Crucifixion: Corpus Hypercubus*, 1954, Salvador Dalí.

'*Diptych: At Matfen/Address to My Daughter*': The Latin tag is from Hebrews 8:13. The KJV is '. . . the same yesterday, and today, and forever'. The phrase in quotation marks is from the Epistle of James 1:17. In the KJV, the entire verse runs 'Every good gift and every perfect gift is from above, and cometh down from the Father of lights, with whom is no variableness, neither shadow of turning.'

'*Diptych: A Holiday in The Western Isles*': John Derry (5 December 1921–6 September 1952) was a De Havilland test pilot famous both for his exceptional flying skills and for being the first British pilot to break the sound barrier. His flying was instrumental in the development of the DH 108 and DH 110 (the forerunner of the Sea Vixen), in which he and his observer, Anthony Richards, were killed when *WG 236* broke up at Farnborough air show due to a structural failure in the outer starboard wing. One of the engines fell onto the tightly packed crowd, killing 29 bystanders. For further information, see Brian Rivas and Annie Bullen, *John Derry: The Story of Britain's First Supersonic Pilot* (William Kimber, 1983; reprinted J. H. Haynes & Co., 2008).

The final line of text in the pages that follow is a fragment from an unpublished poem written in 2001 by J. O. Hudson. The rest of the poem has been lost or destroyed. I reproduce it here in homage to a poem I remember as beautiful, but which no one will read again.

Judgement Judgement Judgement Judgement Judgement Judgememt Judgement
Judgement Judgement Judgement Judgement Judgement Judgememt Judgement
Judgement Judgement Judgement Judgement Judgement Judgememt Judgement
Judgement Judgement Judgement Judgement Judgement Judgememt Judgement
Judgement Judgement Judgement Judgement Judgement Judgememt Judgement
Judgement Judgement Judgement Judgement Judgement Judgememt Judgement
Judgement Judgement Judgement Judgement Judgement Judgememt Judgement
Judgement Judgement Judgement Judgement Judgement Judgememt Judgement
Judgement Judgement Judgement Judgement Judgement Judgememt Judgement
Judgement Judgement Judgement Judgement Judgement Judgememt Judgement
Judgement Judgement Judgement Judgement Judgement Judgememt Judgement
Judgement Judgement Judgement Judgement Judgememt Judgement
Judgement Judgement Judnt Judgememt Judgement
Judgement Judgement Judgememt Judgement
Judgement Judgeme Jgememt Judgement
Judgement Judge ememt Judgement
Judgement Judge memt Judgement
Judgement Judge nemt Judgement
Judgement Judge memt Judgement
Judgement Judge emt Judgement
Judgement Judgem gememt Judgement
Judgement Judgemen udgememt Judgement
Judgement Judgement Jut Judgememt Judgement
Judgement Judgement Judgeement Judgememt Judgement
Judgement Judgement Judgement Judgement Judgement Judgememt Judgement
Judgement Judgement Judgement Judgement Judgement Judgememt Judgement
Judgement Judgement Judgement Judgement Judgement Judgememt Judgement
Judgement Judgement Judgement Judgement Judgement Judgememt Judgement
Judgement Judgement Judgement Judgement Judgement Judgememt Judgement
Judgement Judgement Judgement Judgement Judgement Judgememt Judgement
Judgement Judgement Judgement Judgement Judgement Judgememt Judgement
Judgement Judgement Judgement Judgement Judgement Judgememt Judgement
Judgement Judgement Judgement Judgement Judgement Judgememt Judgement
Judgement Judgement Judgement Judgement Judgement Judgememt Judgement

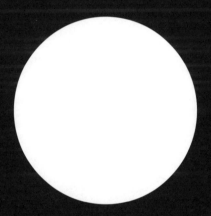

This thing of darkness I acknowledge mine
THE TEMPEST

'Rat,' he found breath to whisper, shaking, 'Are you afraid?'
'Afraid?' murmured the Rat, his eyes shining with unutterable love. 'Afraid?
Of Him? O, never, never. And yet – and yet – O, Mole, I am afraid.'
KENNETH GRAHAME

LET THIS BE YOUR BLIND & FINAL ZEUGMA